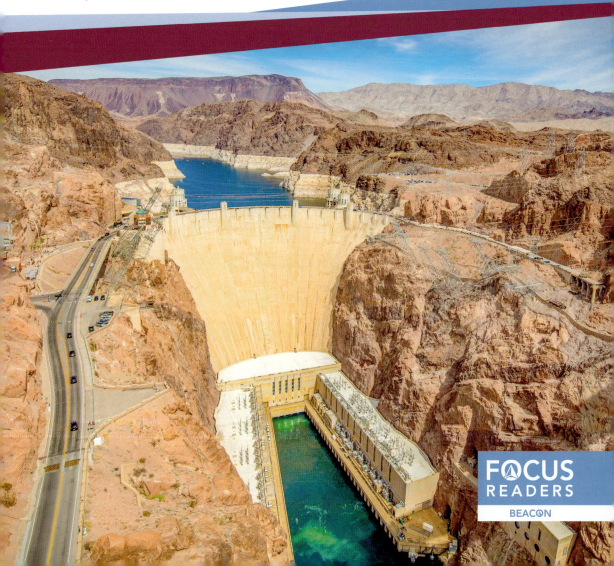

Travel America's Landmarks

Exploring Hoover Dam

by Anita Yasuda

FOCUS READERS

BEACON

www.focusreaders.com

Focus Readers is distributed by North Star Editions:
sales@northstareditions.com | 888-417-0195

Produced for Focus Readers by Red Line Editorial.

Photographs ©: canadastock/Shutterstock Images, cover, 1; hugy/iStockphoto, 4; Red Line Editorial, 7; 4kodiak/iStockphoto, 8; Everett Historical/Shutterstock Images, 11, 12; Jennifer_Sharp/iStockphoto, 14; Alain36/iStockphoto, 17; YinYang/iStockphoto, 19, 29; Nirian/iStockphoto, 20–21; CrackerClips/iStockphoto, 22; RiverNorthPhotography/iStockphoto, 25; thinkreaction/iStockphoto, 27

Library of Congress Cataloging-in-Publication Data
Names: Yasuda, Anita, author.
Title: Exploring Hoover Dam / by Anita Yasuda.
Description: Lake Elmo, MN : Focus Readers, 2020. | Series: Travel America's landmarks | Audience: Grade 4 to 6. | Includes bibliographical references and index.
Identifiers: LCCN 2018060042 (print) | LCCN 2019000531 (ebook) | ISBN 9781641859851 (pdf) | ISBN 9781641859219 (hosted ebook) | ISBN 9781641857833 (hardcover) | ISBN 9781641858526 (pbk.)
Subjects: LCSH: Hoover Dam (Ariz. and Nev.)--History--Juvenile literature. | Dams--Colorado River (Colo.-Mexico)--History--Juvenile literature. | Dams--Design and construction--Juvenile literature.
Classification: LCC TC557.5.H6 (ebook) | LCC TC557.5.H6 Y37 2020 (print) | DDC 627/.820979313--dc23
LC record available at https://lccn.loc.gov/2018060042

Printed in the United States of America
Mankato, MN
May, 2019

About the Author

Anita Yasuda has visited amazing landmarks across North America including Hoover Dam. The author of more than 100 books for children, she lives with her family and her dog on both coasts.

Table of Contents

Chapter 1

Soaring High

A great wall shines in the desert sun. It stretches across a tall canyon. This incredible structure is Hoover Dam. A dam is a wall. It holds back a river's water.

 Hoover Dam blocks the Colorado River to create Lake Mead.

Hoover Dam sits between Arizona and Nevada. It holds back the wild Colorado River. At the foot of the dam is a **power plant**. It uses rushing water to make electricity.

More than seven million people visit Hoover Dam each year. They walk along its length. They gaze over its wide rim. They snap photos

Fun Fact

Hoover Dam was named after President Herbert Hoover.

of the water rushing far below. They also come to marvel at its size. The dam's wall rises 726 feet (221 m). It is taller than the Statue of Liberty.

Chapter 2

The Big Build

For many years, the Colorado River flooded fields and farms. It destroyed **crops**. People wanted a dam built. A large dam could help hold back the river. It could also store water for power.

 The Colorado River crosses seven US states and has created many deep canyons.

Six companies came together to plan and build the dam. They hired **engineer** Frank Crowe to run the project. He had already worked on several other dams.

Starting in 1931, more than 20,000 people came to work on the dam. They first had to move

Fun Fact

Workers had nowhere to live at first. They slept in small tents or cardboard boxes.

 Workers had to climb the canyon walls to build Hoover Dam.

the river around the work site.

Workers used large trucks to drill

into the ground. They dug four large

tunnels. Each tunnel was 56 feet

(17 m) wide. When the tunnels were

finished, the river ran through the

tunnels. It flowed out the other side.

11

 In 1948, Hoover Dam was the world's largest power plant that used the energy of running water.

Workers built the dam with **concrete**. Concrete can be tricky to work with. It becomes hard when it cools down. But it takes a long time to cool. To make it cool more quickly, workers poured wet concrete into blocks. They fitted long pipes into each block. Cold water ran through the pipes. The water helped cool the concrete. The concrete became hard.

Construction finished in 1936. The dam opened to the public. Visitors began arriving.

Fun Fact

Workers used five million barrels of cement. That amount could build a road stretching across the United States!

Chapter 3

Powerful Water

All dams hold back water. But dams can have several different designs. The wall of Hoover Dam is curved. The curve keeps the wall from falling over. It pushes the water to the sides.

 Hoover Dam's curved shape helps the concrete wall stay up.

Hoover Dam holds back the water of the Colorado River. It has kept the Colorado River from flooding since 1936. The water behind the dam forms Lake Mead. The lake is 110 miles (177 km) long. It is one of the largest **reservoirs** in the United States.

Lake Mead has many uses. People come to fish or boat on its open waters. They use water from the lake to wash and cook. Farmers use the water to grow crops.

 Many people visit Lake Mead for fishing, boating, and camping.

A **canal** carries some of the water to California's Imperial Valley. The valley is one of the country's most important farming areas. Most of the fruits and vegetables Americans eat in the winter are grown there.

These foods include melons, corn, and peppers.

The water in Lake Mead is also used for energy. Hoover Dam is one of the biggest **hydroelectric** plants in the United States. Pipes the size of subway tunnels carry water to the dam's power plant. The plant

Fun Fact

California uses approximately 55 percent of all electricity generated by Hoover Dam.

 The generators turn energy from rushing water into electricity.

has 17 large **generators**. They use

the water to make electricity for

1.3 million people.

The Power Plant

Part of Hoover Dam is a power plant. One side of the plant is in Nevada. The other side is in Arizona. The plant uses water from Lake Mead to make electricity. Water flows from the lake into four towers. Each tower stands 395 feet (120 m) high. The water races down pipes into the power plant. As the water falls, it turns large wheels. They are called turbines. The turbines spin generators. They turn the power of rushing water into electricity. Power lines carry the electricity to homes and businesses.

Two towers stand on each side of the canyon.

Chapter 4

Visiting Hoover Dam

Visitors can do many exciting things at Hoover Dam. They can learn about how electricity is made. Visitors can turn a wheel. This action takes physical energy. The energy flows along a wire.

 Hoover Dam visitor center offers tours and has an observation deck.

A bulb lights up. The wheel turns physical energy into electricity.

The visitor center also has old tools used to build the dam. Large black-and-white photos give visitors a peek into the past. They show what the area looked like before the dam was built.

People can explore inside the dam. Visitors take an elevator. They travel down the wall of Black Canyon in only 70 seconds. The wall is more than 500 feet (152 m)

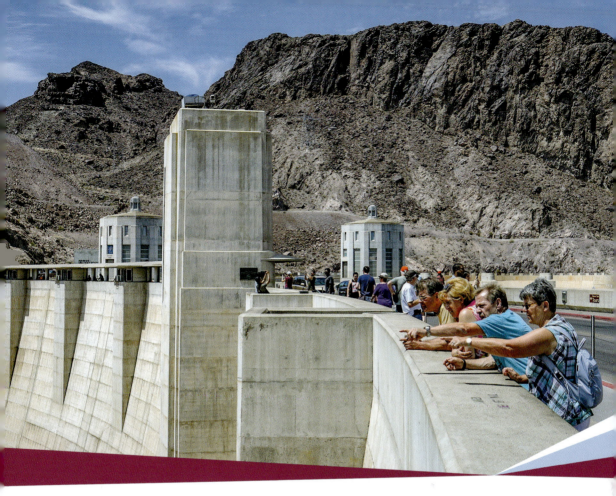

 Visitors can walk along the dam wall and see the Colorado River far below.

deep. In one room, people see eight

of the dam's round generators.

The generators hum and buzz as

they work.

One tunnel inside the dam leads to a large air vent. The vent brings fresh air into the dam. This air helped cool the concrete during the dam's construction. Now people can look out at part of the power plant. It is almost as big as two football fields end to end.

Fun Fact

There are more than 3 miles (4.8 km) of tunnels inside Hoover Dam.

 Hoover Dam provides many of the surrounding areas with electricity.

Today Hoover Dam is a major **landmark**. It reminds people of the skill it took to control the Colorado River. It is also a key source of energy. Electricity from the dam helps power the states of Arizona, Nevada, and California.

Hoover Dam

Write your answers on a separate piece of paper.

1. Write a sentence that describes the key ideas from Chapter 3.

2. Why do you think Hoover Dam is considered a major landmark in the United States?

3. What was the first task that workers had to do in building Hoover Dam?
   - **A.** move the river around the work site
   - **B.** pour the concrete into large blocks
   - **C.** cool down the concrete used for building

4. What might have happened if Hoover Dam had not been built?
   - **A.** The United States would not be able to generate electricity from running water.
   - **B.** The Colorado River would have continued to flood nearby land.
   - **C.** Farmers would have had an easier time growing their crops.

5. What does **designs** mean in this book?

*All dams hold back water. But dams can have several different **designs**. The wall of Hoover Dam is curved.*

    A. shapes

    B. flavors

    C. prices

6. What does **fitted** mean in this book?

*To make it cool more quickly, workers poured wet concrete into blocks. They **fitted** long pipes into each block.*

    A. cut into pieces

    B. removed

    C. put into place

Answer key on page 32.

Glossary

canal
A long, human-made ditch that allows water to flow from one area to another.

concrete
A strong, stonelike material made from gravel, sand, cement, and water.

crops
Plants that are grown for food.

engineer
A person who designs buildings or structures.

generators
Machines that turn the energy of motion into electricity.

hydroelectric
Relating to the generation of electricity with flowing water.

landmark
A place or a building that is easily recognized.

power plant
A place that generates electricity.

reservoirs
Human-made lakes used for water supply storage.

To Learn More

BOOKS

Goldish, Meish. *The Hoover Dam*. New York: Bearport Publishing, 2017.

Jennings, Terry Catasús. *Hydroelectric Energy*. Minneapolis: Abdo Publishing, 2017.

Ringstad, Arnold. *The Building of the Hoover Dam*. Mankato, MN: The Child's World, 2017.

NOTE TO EDUCATORS

Visit **www.focusreaders.com** to find lesson plans, activities, links, and other resources related to this title.

Index

A
Arizona, 6–7, 20, 27

B
Black Canyon, 24

C
California, 17, 18, 27
Colorado River, 6–7, 9,
   16, 27
concrete, 12–13, 26
Crowe, Frank, 10

G
generators, 19, 20, 25

H
Hoover, Herbert, 6

L
Lake Mead, 7, 16, 18, 20

N
Nevada, 6–7, 20, 27

P
power plant, 6, 18, 20, 26

W
workers, 10, 11–12, 13